THE LOEB CLASSICAL LIBRARY

FOUNDED BY JAMES LOEB 1911

EDITED BY

JEFFREY HENDERSON

EDITOR EMERITUS

G. P. GOOLD

CICERO

XII

LCL 309

CICERO

PRO SESTIO
IN VATINIUM

WITH AN ENGLISH TRANSLATION BY

R. GARDNER

HARVARD UNIVERSITY PRESS
CAMBRIDGE, MASSACHUSETTS
LONDON, ENGLAND

ISBN 0-674-99341-1

*Printed in Great Britain by St Edmundsbury Press Ltd,
Bury St Edmunds, Suffolk, on acid-free paper.
Bound by Hunter & Foulis Ltd, Edinburgh, Scotland.*

CONTENTS

PREFACE

Many years ago I accepted an invitation from the
Editors of the Loeb Classical Library to revise and
complete the five speeches of Cicero now comprised in
two volumes, a work which had been left unfinished
by their contributor, the late J. H. Freese, M.A.,
formerly Fellow of St. John's College, Cambridge,
and Assistant Master at Repton School and at St.
Paul's School. His earlier contribution to the Loeb
Library was a volume published in 1930 which con-
tained Cicero's speeches *Pro P. Quinctio*, *Pro Sex.
Roscio Amerino*, *Pro Q. Roscio Comoedo*, and *De lege
agraria, i-iii.*

I regret that the completion of this task has been
gravely interrupted and delayed by the claims of
administrative work and other duties. It is, however,
possible that some advantage may have been gained
by this delay. Within the last generation scholars
have assiduously investigated the wealth of literary
evidence that has made political and prosopographical
studies of the late Roman Republic so profitable a
field of inquiry. Their labours have thrown new light
upon some aspects of the setting and the subject-
matter of Cicero's speeches. To these recent re-

PREFACE

searches and, no less, to those of earlier date, I have been under a constant obligation. The Bibliography which will be found on pp. 353-360 is, naturally, far from exhaustive ; it is no more than a list of such books and articles as have been found useful in the preparation of these volumes, and may indicate the amount of work which has been done in this field. My chief debt is to those annotated editions without whose aid I could have done nothing. Over seventy years have passed since two of them were published : J. S. Reid's edition of the *Pro Balbo* appeared in 1878, H. A. Holden's edition of the *Pro Sestio* in 1883. Two are more recent. In 1924 H. E. Butler and M. Cary published their edition of the *De provinciis consularibus*, and L. G. Pocock's edition of the *In Vatinium* is dated to 1926. The most recent commentary on the *Pro Caelio* is Professor R. G. Austin's revision (1952) of his earlier work (1933). For the guidance and help which I have received from this indispensable work I am obviously indebted and I am deeply grateful.

I have departed but rarely from the text used by the original translator, the Teubner edition (1904) by C. F. W. Müller, and then only to adopt suggestions by editors of the annotated editions. Müller's text has now been superseded by the Teubner edition of 1919 by A. Klotz and F. Schöll.

In any assessment of the qualities of the Ciceronian corpus these five speeches, taken as a whole, must be judged worthy of a high place. They not only vividly illustrate some of those literary qualities which

viii